THE REASON BEHIND POLITICS

ii

DANIEL UWITONZE

iii

Active discernment towards political scenarios will let us know the purpose of the incident action and determine our best behavior in every situation. It's good to consider why this? To discover political reality and motive to determine how we behave in society

Copyright

Dedication

iii

To anyone who wishes to discover political reality and motive to determine how we behave in society.

DANIEL UWITONZE

DANIEL UWITONZE

INTRODUCTION

Everything is politically motivated. Many hypocrites are behind what we see with naked eyes. That is a great card mostly played by politicians; here, they can create a good or evil act with sound effects that will bring what they want.

Active discernment towards political scenarios will let us know the purpose of the incident action and determine our best behavior in every situation. It's good to consider why this? To discover political reality and motive to determine how we behave in society. As a result, we will self-regulate when and what to say, do, hear and see.

After all, a wise person, before making a decision and judgment, should ask oneself the following questions:

1. Why is this happening?
2. What is the mission and impact of the scenario?

(Those questions should be the concern for everyone; be the politician and subordinates.) After providing the answers to the above questions, it is when we should start deciding and judging the scene. This is what Jesus said:

"Before you speak, turn your tongue seven times." This means we have to spend that time thinking and asking the questions that will give us the needed information, meaning, and answers to make the right decision. Simply take enough time to consider before we open our mouth to speak or do anything.

The wise person, before making a decision and judgment, should ask himself the following questions:

3. Why is this happening?

4. What is the mission and impact of the scenario? After providing the answers to the above questions, it is when we should start deciding and judging the scene. This is what Jesus said: "Before you speak, turn your tongue seven times." This means we have to spend that time thinking and asking the questions that will give us the needed information, meaning, and answers to make the right decision. Simply take enough time to consider before we open our mouth to speak. You should remember, in real life, everything has a connection with politics.

POLITICS IS OUR DAILY LIFE

We have to accept that politics is a part of everything we see in this life. How you behave is determined by the politics of your country and region of origin or by your politics. Whether your life is rich or poor is all about the effects of the political turmoil. Mind that your ideas and beliefs are the political pictures of your origin, and everything is based on the political principles set by our predecessors.

It is why the behavior of an American differs from that of a Chinese; Europeans' behavior is different from Africans', and the People of Saudi Arabia may vary in culture from the people of Italy. They are all determined by the politics in a given area.

Politics is for everyone's livelihood; that is why everyone should become the first political partner in a particular country or region. So ignoring your role in the country's development makes you feel that this is the job of politicians, yet good politics will solve your problems.

Times change forever, as these priests often say when they read the gospel; this is the unchanging truth. In ordinary life without many numbers involved, you go up and down; we laugh, but tomorrow you cry; we rejoice today, and tomorrow we are in pain.

We give birth, and we lose our beloved ones, but we give birth again, we go to bed and wake up, we eat and be satisfied, but soon we are hungry; we are loved now, but later on, they will hate us, but this is the world. In short, living in this world requires constantly being prepared for each change and learning to accept each one that happens to us; the good news is remembering that it will have an end.

This is why we should choose to have a little fun, not by being happy forever. Let's rejoice but discerning that we hurt none; we should not keep in the joy to forget always to be prepared for the bad times that may be hiding behind the pleasure we have right away. Also, we should not be overwhelmed by the sorrow of forgetting the many good things that have happened to us and what awaits us.

It would be a pity to be surprised by problems that you may have been well prepared for, but you be surprised by just being busy in happy times. It is like a farmer who reaps the harvest in a time of enormous production, then eats and spends the yield wastefully, forgetting to store it for the next famine. A particular country can have peace and security due to severe injuries after stopping the enemy by severely weakening its enemy or even harshly pushing them back to provide sustainable peace and tranquility to the people.

Time passes so that there is a great deal of sleep; the people fail to be the eyes of the country; they associate with anyone present, including the enemy, and the security guards over-eat and over-drunk, marry and reproduce more, and sleep and oversleeping. So the country stays in everlasting joy, and the enemy re-enters and seizes the country or fails but brings it back in the bad times, and the happiness ends, and security and peace end.

It is not wrong to celebrate victory, but it is a mistake for certain citizens of any country who has lived through a difficult period of war to forget. And they fall asleep and neglect everything that has plagued the country in the difficult times it has gone through. No government exists without an enemy, so ignoring borders to prevent enemies from outside the country is a big mistake that any country should not make. There should also be good relations with possible countries for information and aid that helps a country to develop in many ways, including overcoming the enemy of growth.

It is even more important to hold accountable and maintain justice and security by identifying, retrieving, or suppressing potential threats within Countries. I can assure you that if one or two of the above is ignored, I am sure it will cost such Countries, the cost that can even put Countries back in the worst of times or bring another worse situation than the first.

The above explains why a superpower country cannot make a single mistake that can reverse it from being a world common denominator. Even if countries themselves are sufficiently secure, they will do their best to keep their troops in serious training until they engage themselves to manage security in other war-torn countries. They intend to get used to the war and its tactics so that, at some point, they will have enough practical skills to defend themselves from future tragedy. I do not doubt that their soldiers are involved in many wars, but currently, these countries have rarely experienced civil wars. Tactically, it will be well illustrated with domestic and foreign training after studying the war on paper. Above all, if a particular country has no domestic rebel attacks or no civil war, the government may learn about the realities of the enemy or the threat to peace in another specific country.

What is needed is adequate military training, which is not just about staying on paper; at some point, a given country may invent the enemy. Discovering the battle's tricks and believing your theoretical skills will require meeting the enemy on the front lines on the battlefield. After all, it is on the battlefield that military capabilities are being revealed, and the presence of trained soldiers and modern and capable military equipment determines this. Not only does this mean fighting in every way to practice your skills, but it also means that when it comes to defending, protecting, and fighting for innocent others, it is also a way to show that you are capable in military operations.

After theoretical studies of war, there must be tactical and practical training through real battlegrounds. In addition, the soldiers get used to practical tactics during a real fight. On a battlefield, the soldiers may plan to attack and face an enemy or a terrorist of a country or try to restore peace in a certain war-torn country or region. This has led to the fact that if they have not learned about the war in war-torn country A, they learned it in the same country named B. Maybe on a peace mission, their troops got tactical and practical war missions elsewhere, with no mistake, but the soldiers should get enough training. Those troops in other countries may be there for the right peacekeeping mission, training, international security partnership, or invading mission, even though there may be another mission behind what is in official papers.

Think twice and be wise about the reason behind every scene of military operations in other countries. As I have often said, restoring peace and defeating the enemy of the country, military training, military cooperation, and helping the oppressed or fighting for friendship are the missions of war in another country. The fact is that a country without war has no choice but to gain experience in foreign wars would be better for both sides benefiting in a win-and-win situation. It is not suitable for the country to be quiet as if it has no enemies and stays joyful, regardless of the changes that can occur.

As you go along, you will understand the purpose and meaning of each activity you see being done by the state; none of them which are not politically motivated and happen without cause, and that reason is understandable and pre-designed. But, unfortunately, it is of shame to find some of them which may be deliberately done to the detriment of the public interest for the benefit of one person, family, or party. Here, it becomes more dangerous when there is a hidden or open hand that helps to disrupt security in a particular country. The support comes from the one hand on the left, but the right hand is ready to receive praise and glory with many benefits. Sometimes it is an incomparable benefit to the aid provided, and even if the aid may have cost innocent blood, even if it is of one person, no one can make the one back to life.

Much of what politics does is control our emotions and end up having a positive or negative impact on our lives. Everything that the leaders of the world do intends for our minds, and our minds command the body to do everything. It also means that politics understands how to bring about its aspirations for the desired change in the individual or society. People's attitudes often coincide with the politics of a particular region or country.

Life seems like a great lesson won by someone who knows how to control this world and human emotions. The only thing that has been able to handle this is politics, and someone who uses politics is a politician. This one (politician) also controls the world and the people's emotions, either positively or negatively. Be cautious!

This one has learned to control the human mind and all the behaviors this world shows. Politics has transformed the world, brought people together, divided people, established languages, separated the continents, and built the borders of nations. Politicians demolished a lot, and his hands can change everything. At the beginning of his plan, you could see the one play like a little child but with a great mission to achieve.

I talked to my grandfather about a white priest who owned, which differed from what Religion taught. He said, "I had a white master who owned a monkey," which is very popular with girls and women. He kept telling me more about the story "The monkey escaped from my enslaver and saw a woman carrying a baby, the monkey started fighting with the woman, and people came to save her.

The monkey picked up the baby and climbed the tree with the baby. People kept shouting, and the monkey grabbed the baby and hit him on the wooden tree, and he died. Shortly afterward, a white priest came and took his gun and shot his monkey. The people said, "he (the priest) caused problems, and now he is the one who solved it, but the child was dead!"

He concluded, "My point was that there was another reason that was hiding behind the Religion because he was there teaching and preaching about Bible, but he also had a mining project to represent. They (colonizers) knew that some owning people would not be happy for them. Some people intended to oppose colonizers, which would lead the priest to possess more weapons than the word of God from the Bible. So, this favored the wise man that he would not oppose them because opposing those equals being expelled or betrayed to death," he said. Thinking about it helps you to think about what might be hidden behind each activity because what you see as good but not all of them have a positive effect.

Only no document has shown that colonialism intended to enlighten Africa as a real cause. It is because the inequality between Africa and other continents had increased even more than before when Africa was still in the so-called darkness. Where we do not yet have a civilization, Africa is considered the poorest continent as opposed to the pre-colonial one. It refers to the changes in practices and beliefs of Africans, each of which has been revised like traditional languages, Religion, education and training, and governance. Everything that goes in the way they want is also what makes the influence visible even now because we seem to imitate, and by imitating, it is hard to be perfect than the one who taught you.

Today, traditional African languages are not popular to quickly help an African to work in European countries; the person needs to learn either English or french. Even it isn't easy to perform better in your country of origin with your traditional language. If you want to succeed, at least learn English or French because that is how you will be heard and recognized by many, even your fellow Africans with whom you share the same nationality.

The positive thinking about this makes you feel that what is right is sticking and promoting yours when you see it gives you peace and development and lets it become your specialty. But when you find yourself failing, change and start using what you have found in others, then do it as well as yours because if they bring it to you, it will be costly. Its specialty will come with viable changes to differentiate you from the owner. That helps the individual, region, country, or continent to absorb the existing and make it ultimately themselves without claiming it from other countries.

The world we live in today is so focused on the development and politics of war that some see the truth of what is happening and clearly understand its reality. The question is, who should know the truth and who will determine it? What power do they have to choose the truth? In this world, the fact known to many is likely worthless, maybe because they are not the ones to determine the truth. Sometimes, the majority can fail to tell the truth. However, we believe that most people usually agree on what should be true when they accept it; this is part of Democracy.

Remember that at that time, those present were saying, "Crucify Him!" Who is that? Jesus. Pilatus has already seen no trial against Jesus; people have said that although he has no guilt for crucifixion. The people shouted, "We would rather be given Barabbas a thief in those days, but Jesus hanged at the cross." That did not mean they were telling the truth, but Pilatus was nothing more than accepting to crucify Jesus; it was a truth agreed upon and confirmed by many.

In Democracy, it is good to let people make their choice, but there should always be a need for selected people to analyze some of those many deeply. Then, that group of people has to directly govern people's choices so that decisions are not made wrongly. Here, it is to avoid poor and low-informed decision-making's negative and severe consequences.

The previously stated means that there is always a lot of information needed to make a decision, which is why one should first think about the reason and mission that may be hidden behind the action before one decide. It is vital to make a healthy decision. So before we take any action on the scene right now, we must first gather enough information to get us to the exact reason behind what we are going to be involved with and in.

I have come up with some strong examples of past acts to guide and give you the time to think about the rest of the history that this book did not cover. All will help you go deeper into such events to find the reasons behind them and the people behind each action. Sometimes, we think that some actions took/take place by accident; my purpose is to tell you how and why too many activities occur intentionally and have been planned before they will happen to benefit or harm someone else.

QUALITIES OF GOOD POLITICS

You need to know how to fulfill your responsibilities in everything you do. Let this cost you whatever possible to achieve your responsibilities perfectly. After all, it is honesty and Heroism to fulfill your given commitment. Do this well in relationships, family and relatives, religion, leadership, and other responsibilities.

If you are in a position of responsibility, you should keep it in mind so that those responsibilities dominate all your actions. It would be best to prioritize such duties more than your agenda. Remember that is where God wanted and allowed you to help His people. Doing so is not only pleasing to the people but also pleasing to God. That is why you are in that position; do not guess the other reason why!

Be responsible and do not fight to change who you are, the one who made them trust you, because if you lose your originality, it will show that you have disappointed them, and they will see that you do not deserve those responsibilities. Keep the same person. Those, as mentioned earlier, will give you an uphill climb until, at the top of the mountain, you will always have some valid reasons for them to believe that you are the right one.

Avoid tricks as much as possible to make yourself feel better or stronger. Because pranks may hurt someone and the one will always want revenge, it will take time for that person will achieve his revenge action on you. So if you live longer, be prepared to see the anger from the wounds left behind.

In all the responsibilities you have or will be in, remember that all the strength you have has come from those who trusted you and therefore strive to persuade not to deceive them in deeds; stop words but do them. After all, a person should be lifted and raised so that he can take others where we are not, which is precisely the goal we have in common.

So where you are, if you remember that we have you in our hands, do what we have sent you to do because that is your purpose, and that is why we cannot give up because you are fulfilling your responsibilities. Our joy in seeing you achieve something else that will benefit us makes us truly unbreakable for the good that we expect from you.

Ignoring your responsibilities at the top, being lazy, being selfish, what you achieve is only yours and keeps consuming ours; these make you heavier and can make us put you down in any way that can break you! All will depend on your heaviness. We should recognize the attraction force of the earth to rely on his ability to reach, to be, and stay up there. People are the only ones who agree to take someone and raise him to give that person joy and benefit them. Remember that it is easy to fall down and that you may always stay on the ground because of the earth's attraction power; without humans, we are nothing. After all, birds are not always in the air, they fly away and come down on the ground, and they will die on the floor.

Imagine in a starving moment people are together, and they see a tree with a lot of fruit. The tree is so large that no one can hug it, and the seeds are so large that no man's height can reach the fruit even if he stretches out his arms. The people immediately went together and discussed, and the ideas became more and more, but they were hungry. God found them there in a meeting and gave them the idea that they should take one and put him up to take and bring fruits. People start thinking about someone they can post that above. And they found the right one to be sent above.

Let me start by commenting on the idea shared above. Hungry people mean the lives of people and the problems they have and always need to be solved. People should always go together and start looking for solutions to their problems. There must always be a leader who meets all the requirements to guide them in getting what they want. A leader should go there through the election, as in the idea they put someone up to bring fruit for the rest. The fat tree and the distant fruit are the challenges people face when they go to find solutions, allowing them to choose someone to whom they give the power to help them overcome those challenges.

Transparent elections are the only way to find a good and trustworthy person who must lead others. In the joys of being at the top, remember you are there for an excellent mission to the people; understandably, the above glory and pride can be sought by anyone. Remember, there are people on the ground who are breaking, and those you hurt are the ones who chose you to be up.

After all, one who is mentally and physically strong and fearless, someone who is aware of the reason to be up, who knows the purpose, who is humble, and who accepts the opinions of others. Remember that among those you left down, there are young ones, older people, and sick people who need your help, but more importantly, there may be others who can replace you.

Of all the responsibilities, first and foremost, ask yourself that, "What do I need to do to fulfill my responsibilities"? Take the family as an example; if you have family responsibilities, first find out what you are like in the family. For example, if you are a parent, you are required to take care of your spouse, especially your children, and get to know each other. You should also be aware that your family needs you as much as possible without neglecting family and friends who need help. Adhering to this is enough to fulfill other responsibilities because every child deserves compassion like yours.

To choose a leader, you need to look at the right person who will meet many of the following; Humbleness/Humility, Mission adherence, Flexibility, Selfless, Fearlessness, and Truthfulness.

1. Humility:

All elections have their basis, and people vote based on human capacity. Someone gets there and harvests the seeds because people came together and raised someone above in their hands. All in all, seek to fulfill your responsibilities until you mandate is over; the people will still be there for you without being tired of you.

To prevent fatigue, they will probably set up a person who is not overweight (**Not too heavy person**).

Every leader should be humble, with all the characteristics preventing them from weighing people down. After all, the leader's heavy weight will make them fail so quickly that they will put him on the ground without achieving their goal.

2. Mission adherence:

Either way, people will vote for someone as hungry as they are and who has started a journey with them and with the same originality. It is someone who knows exactly how the problem started and understands the existing challenges. That person should also look for positive change and understand and accept the conventional way to find solutions. Finally, that person should be the one who wants the most answers to the problems and challenges that exist. It is best to feel the same issue and enjoy the same answers as others because it makes you think about what they need.

3. Flexibility.

Remember that the person they are going to put up is someone whom they will withstand and tolerate his heaviness. Here, in turn, makes it easier for the person to be humble in everything. In the same way, it is essential to be humble and responsive to everyone's needs without discrimination. When you don't have that flexibility, you end up burdening the people who put you in charge, and this would make them relinquish responsibility because you are breaking them for nothing.

4. Selfless and empathy:

The person in charge must also be aware of the number of others. He should not be selfish, and everything he wants should be good for others. One should not reap the fruit for oneself but should give them to the others on the ground so they may later share the fruits. If you are a leader, you must feel the people's burden and work hard to fulfill your promises.

5. Fearlessness:

The top is scary, so the one who should go there is the one who is not scared. That is also a baseless fear because when you do your job well, the people who hold you will keep you from falling to the ground. Under any leadership, this should not be confused as a time of happiness, but a fearsome position of responsibility. You may have to deal with problems whenever you do your responsibility poorly, so you have to fear.

However, if you fulfill your obligations, you will not be intimidated. Remember that getting up and being scared will prevent you from doing your job well; stop being scared. So often, many people are afraid of responsibility. Finding someone who accepts responsibility for the common good is an opportunity people should pay attention to during the election.

6. Trustfulness:

That person should also be trustworthy in words and deeds. Hope gives peace, tranquility, and unwavering support to the person you have provided to achieve your responsibilities. People always believe that someone will bring what he has been sent for. When it comes down to trustfulness, the voters should be conscientious. Some of them may have a more trustworthy person, which may be due to emotional or other factors. This is why a leader should be trusted by more than one person and gets such trust through proper actions without other emotions from love or family background.

VIEW OF POLITICS IN DIVERSITY

Politics has a vital role in showing the advantages of differences because politics has played a role in division and discrimination. Diversity has been the key to greatness in world politics and throughout history. There are people we know who are famous in their history for hating certain people and killing them until they want to make them disappear from the earth. There are other people we know in the history of the world who have faced discrimination and become role models for people around the world.

Historical books of philosophers and religious books spoke of differences; some people use/used them to bring divisions among people, but others use/used them to fight divisions and bring unity and reconciliation among people. Politics has led to people openly expressing their hatred towards other people; it also allows for other people who do not express hatred in their speech, but their hearts are so divided; but the good thing is that there are people who are not divided in their hearts.

The difference is the factor that makes good politics and bad politics appear; the point that every politician should show people how one will handle and control the differences. We all have something to write about this topic because, depending on our political background, we have how we met diversity challenges.

It is possible that inside your heart, you feel hatred and discrimination, or you feel in your heart that you do not hate and discriminate; I want to tell you that it all depends on the governance background of your region or country. Political differences led some to become evil killers to commit Genocide, and millions of lives were lost; however, good politics stop Genocide and other discrimination-based killings

Some people have turned into animals that walk like blind people, and in front of them, some wise men and scholars lead people to murder instead of bringing them a better life; this is bad politics; however, some people enlighten others and bring them to unity and reconciliation, which leads to development and good life, this is good politics.

Because of the differences, politics has made some gods and others enslaved people until people treat others as their gods. Inequality has resulted in some people being enslaved, devalued, and sold like any other commodity. However, we always see good people who fight against division, racism, and discrimination because they know that despite having different traits and missions, we are all human; that differences are united to benefit people.

Undoubtedly, facing differences is the greatest struggle that human beings are constantly engaged in; some fight for human rights, unity, peace, and reconciliation and do it internationally for a united world. This idea led to the establishment of international organizations to prevent and stop conflicts in families, among the people of a particular country, and between certain nations so that we do not return to murder, discrimination, genocide, or another world war.

All those are being done, but it is also productive in some places, but you see, people are dying because of their race in other places. Inequality, discrimination, and division seem to have become chronic diseases among people; the strange thing is that an antidote is available and always given, but people refuse to provide it or take it respectively; maybe this is because of negligence or other attached benefits. It is often caused by toxic speeches that spread hatred from very toxic people, and ordinary people listen to them and change to the point where they can no longer listen to other communities with a cure.

Sometimes you can find someone so severely damaged that it is impossible to bring one back online. Divisions often occur because many people listen and overthink negative things, especially when an influential person like a politician speaks to them. That can lead people to follow what is being said unconsciously to the point where they become terrible people.

However, the voice of people who call others to end the division is devalued and ignored; every person who fights for peace should know that more power is required than the power of the people who destroy it. For it is known that to destroy is easy, but to build is difficult; so if you strive for unity and reconciliation, stand up without fear because doing it lazily increases the intensity of the enemy of peace.

It is evident that whenever people come together to fight against evil, the evil becomes defeated because God always supports them because they are fighting for the truth. As long as protection seems impossible, stopping the division requires effort and dedication; even a person could accept dying, as the following examples show.

Remember the slavery in the United States of America; from 1861 to 1864, it required Abraham Lincoln to fight against slavery, and it is believed that he was the one who stopped it and made the African

American society start to have freedom. Nelson Mandela fought against apartheid in South Africa until he was imprisoned for 27 years.

Martin Luther King Jr. fought for civil and black Americans' rights from 1955 until he was killed in 1968. From 1944 to 1945, the United Nations was able to stop the Genocide of the Jews and stop the Second World War. It happened in Rwanda in 1994 when Rwandans came together from different countries they had fled to and came to liberate and stop the Genocide against the Tutsis that was being carried out in the country. Many people became victims to stop the Genocide and restore peace to the country.

If you look at history, many sacrifices and efforts have been made to achieve peace. Because of the corrupt world, peace remains more precious than other things; some people sacrifice themselves to achieve lasting peace for others. I tell you the truth that the fight against slavery in the world, especially in the USA, required sacrifices before and after President Abraham Lincoln; even also Lincoln was shot dead in 1865.

Because of the great power used by people who bring divisions among people, fighting against them also requires many times more energy than theirs to restore peace. It is a struggle that requires a person to care about the outcome even if one will no longer alive, as shown by the words of some of those who fought for peace.

On this subject, Mandela said,

"I have cherished the ideal of a democratic and free society in which all persons live together in harmony and with equal opportunities. It is an ideal that I hope to live for and achieve. But if needs be, it is an ideal for which I am prepared to die."

To this day, many people are still searching and fighting for their rights; I am telling you that if you are fighting for the truth, you will win; even though not all of you will achieve it, your descendants will be at peace.

On the other hand, a living person is a person who knows that s/he will die, and that makes someone does good while still alive until one's death becomes life for many other people. If this doesn't happen, you will end up dead, and the world will remain in trouble for nothing you did to save it.

Imagine existing in the world and doing evil, sowing hatred among people until you die; even after your death, you leave evil deeds that will harm creatures; let none of us become like these people.

Abraham Lincoln said, "In the end, it is not the years in your life that count. It is the life in your years".

So the question is, "What have I been doing for so long? Did what I did solve the problem people were having? After all, there is no choice; a person should do good things until s/he completes one's mission on earth. Whenever you enjoy the bad things you do and force us to accept your choices in society, you should know that you are damaged and need a cure.

Striving for peace and living a peaceful life is bravery; you don't need to do good while you are still alive so that we will always remember you, but to be personally brave and proud of the good deed of love that you do even in the face of death, is bravery beyond measure. Although we remember heroes, there are heroes we don't know; there may be a person, who was killed together with people someone was trying to save, and there was no one to testify, but nothing will remove the fact that you are brave, even if we don't know your details. All of you who fight for peace, unity, and reconciliation everywhere deserve more than the Noble peace prize.

Explaining the impact of the division as a Rwandan would not be entirely wrong. Rwanda is an excellent example of the effects of division and the benefits of promoting unity and reconciliation. It is a well-known fact that when a wise person is someone who faced with a problem and gets out of it with lessons, that person starts to take measures to avoid returning to such a dire situation again.

It may require stable security, unity and reconciliation, and a stable economic strategy that will lead to sustainable development. We also don't need to face challenges to take lessons; mistakes made elsewhere can also teach us. After all, it is not necessary to learn from the mistakes you made, but a wise person learns from the mistakes of others and avoids making the same mistakes because that person knows what it costs.

If you know something that burned down your neighbor's house, would you end up owning that thing? It is essential and instructive that you learn from the mistakes that led to Genocide in a specific country and thus ensure that there will be no Genocide in your country. Observing and analyzing carefully what caused certain countries to fight can make you live better with your neighbors.

So you think the politicians don't know what caused the world wars and their consequences? A person who does not know the causes of tragedies and their effects should not be a politician. The problem is that some leaders know very well the causes and impacts of conflict but want to use the same way to destroy the masses of people. People should sit down and remember their human connection and then unite.

The destruction of conflict should characterize people's negotiations leading to peace; they should end by looking together at the common enemy humans have created, climate change. Otherwise, one or all would be committed to accepting the loss of lives due to conflict. Humanism makes a person a good politician who is concerned about public issues and does so for the benefit of all and the protection of the environment.

Diversity is a source of development. The development of the country is not only in one aspect; imagine finding a country with a well-built city, but you find that most of the people in the country are hungry and have no security there; it is not developed because it does not integrate many aspects including health, education, and security.

To achieve personal development, a person must have different factors which contribute to physical, financial, relational, emotional, spiritual, and intellectual. Of course, you need many things and different people to contribute to your progress. You will not get all aspects from one place or thing and will not be developed in only one part.

All this, as I wrote, is what a good politician cares about and does not discriminate in order to have a prosperous people. However, some disrupt others' peace and all means of achieving development because of their culture or ethnicity. Because of the above aspects make people completely different; you find that a person does not look like another in every physical appearance, white and black or Asian, tall or short by height, and other physical traits, but the person remains human.

Some people are different from others in terms of their finances, one is really rich, and the other is poor, but they are all called people. You will find that others have different behavior concerning others, and this is where a person can be a peacemaker, and another is a person who divides others; Also, people are different in how they feel and express their emotions.

Some people are different spiritually, and you may find that our beliefs are different, but we are all human; this is also the case in terms of mental and intellectual differences; you may find that one person has a big difference from another in terms of mentality, but they are all human.

All this, as I have already shown, explains the difference between one person and another because it makes one have different attitudes and perspectives from another. The only problem is that some people have bad differences because of life experiences that have caused their personal development aspects to deteriorate, and they also deteriorate. It doesn't matter how different people are because it allows people to make various contributions to the development of everyone they meet.

Members of the same church may have spiritual, which is somehow closer, yet their thinking, financial capability, emotions, and relationships are different. It also allows for various thoughts, and you find people who like separate things; this makes people with many talents come from a particular family or country.

Life in ordinary families is where one child knows how to clean the house, but you find another who knows how to cook and loves it; however you may find another who loves and has the strength to go with ones parents to find food for the family, So all of them are united in what they like and can do for a prosperous family.

So it is with the country's development; People who like the profession of teaching will become teachers and professors, making education better in the country. Others who want a job in medicine will become doctors and nurses, which will make people's lives better maintained. The same is true of people who study engineering; they become good engineers.

It is also the case with people who feel called to preach as religious leaders who help people to develop spiritually. That is how a good family needs to raise a child in both aspects so that tomorrow one will contribute to the country's and the world's development. And the government should have young people who have these healthy values to believe in the country's future.

Imagine a child born hearing parents telling him or her that s/he should not live with others because they do not share the same race, ethnicity, religion, or culture, and even find the leaders themselves support it. And when he comes to religion, they teach him that he should not live with others who do not pray together in the same church. He gets the same hate experience in sports and entertainment; I'm telling you, he's so messed up that there's nothing evil he's afraid to do, and he will bring a negative difference in society.

But unlike a child born to be taught love by parents, he gets the same love stories at school. When he comes to the temple, he finds that they teach peace and love, so even in games and entertainment, he finds that there is no division; this child will grow up to make a positive difference in society.

Sometimes people differ because some show positive differences, and others show negative ones.

However, you should know that the people who show significant differences; contribute according to their different packages and help build the country in various aspects.

Politics that understand diversity and inclusiveness develop the country. After the Genocide against Tustis in Rwanda in 1994, it was quite possible that the nation would remain in a bad situation if the politics of unity and reconciliation did not come. Many different things have been done to get the country back on track.

One of them is to give everyone a chance to contribute to building a new nation. It was also done regardless of race and ethnicity, and the program of unity and reconciliation was sped up so that divisions did not slow progress or destroy achievements. Indeed, Rwanda has not reached as far as it wants, but where it came from is very far, so the big difference was seen a little while ago due to good politics that draws shared benefit from diversity. Continuing such a line would lead Rwandans to the desired long-term development.

You will be successful if you avoid divisions and welcome different perspectives in improving people's lives. After all, America and other countries have different kinds of people; their growth and strength depend on diversity. In this way, what one cannot do, the other can do, making their decision stronger and wiser. Imagine a country with many people representing most countries; this itself is an extraordinary strength in personnel, security, and international relations.

On the other hand, some countries have failed to treat a difference for the common good; that is the bad politics I was talking about, characterized by tyranny, robbery, inequality, and division, so the country is constantly at war, they are busy killing each other, destroying what they have built, robbery finds an entry point, and the nation ends up in poverty.

Therefore, people who know the benefits of diversity should always teach others about it to have a peaceful world. If it is not done, there will be another reason behind it. It would be a mistake of global discrimination characterized by understanding that good things are only suitable for certain people so that others remain like they are so that we continue to be different in capability.

I want to talk to you, the person reading this book; let's ignore the politics and everything else about it. Are we really supposed to accept and implement everything we hear without thinking? It is unfortunate that someone would lead us on the wrong path, and we would follow one blindly until we become cruel people. I continued to say that we are all human because we have humanity; so don't let anyone make you lose your humanity. We should always purify our thoughts; we listen carefully and observe the things that can lead us out of the right line.

Also, you and I should always have a word ready to say in response to anyone who brings division and discrimination. If someone tells you that you don't look like someone, reply, "Even I and you are different, but the difference should make us join together;" you should add, "But above all, we are all human." Maybe someone else will come and tell you, "You are different from another in culture and behavior;" say to him, "I already know, and it doesn't matter," adding that "That one may probably have more humanity than us and that makes him someone we should learn from."

Maybe someone will come and remind you of evil things and say, "How dare you live with that person who killed your family and betrayed you?" you will answer him, "I forgave him so that I myself could live," and add, "I forgave him because a revengeful life nothing would benefit my descendants and my country; that is the contributive difference I have to give to the society."

Maybe someone will tell you that you are black and completely different from white; you should answer, "I know, but I realized that none of us have something that makes us more human than others; if we all still have humanity, then we are all human."

Good politics always comes with many reminders that diversity is not a problem; you will see this when the certain government brings different games and entertainment. International sports and entertainment competitions bring together people from many countries; this is when people put aside their differences to compete, but please people watching them physically and online. However, this is also the time to assess whether the world has recovered from the communicable disease of racism, discrimination and division.

Let me talk about different games; some people love and play sports together; one may like football and the other likes basketball. However, when it comes down to the type of game, you will find that people who love football are fans of different clubs and countries' teams.

I talked with my friend Moses; we mentioned the football clubs we support worldwide, starting in our country. We found ourselves supporting two different clubs in the country, but when I asked about his club in England, we all found ourselves fans of the same club. We continued to talk about our team, and I found out that he had favorite players, which I didn't really like; but when a player scored a goal, we all cheered. Even though we have many differences, what is needed is to succeed. Incredibly, we meet again in the World Football Cup, supporting the same national team, different from the country where there are our fun clubs.

This is the life where a person you do not meet in sports will meet at work, church, or association, and you may even find yourself living in the same place. Do those make people fight? Let's not ignore the fact that people can share the country, so if you want to bring divisions from inside or outside the country, we will tell you that we are all Rwandans, we are Congolese, we are Chinese, we are Americans, and other names like all the countries of the world are. And if an enemy from among us tells us that we are different, tell him we are all human wherever we are.

This brings me to the story I wanted to tell you. After Rwanda emerged from the terrible times of the Genocide, there were many Genocide survivors and many wounded people. Revenge was possible, but the politics of unity and reconciliation started, as I explained in the above pages. However, this did not stop some people from continuing their ideology inside and outside the country. Slogan became a response to give anyone who brings divisions "NDUMUNYARWANDA (I AM RWANDAN)," which was done inside and outside the country and produced results because it dissolved into the blood of all people, especially the youths.

I remember a friend of mine, Vincent, who fell in love with a girl named Judith, and they didn't really care about anything, but as time passed, they got to talking about the country's history. Vincent came to know that Judith lives with her grandmother, who is a survivor of the Genocide against Tutsis in Rwanda; Vincent didn't care about that so much because he was aware that his family did not commit Genocide.

They agreed to visit each other starting with Judith; Judith told the boy, "When you get our home, be patient because my grandmother may ask you questions and scare you, but don't worry because I love you and am determined to be with you." Then Vincent replied, "There is no problem, my love," but there was a little fear in his heart; he had a lot of curiosity mixed with fear, wondering what the old lady would ask him.

Finally, the right time came, and Vincent arrived at Judith's family and found that many girls were waiting for him and singing a song thanking him for taking the step to love Judith and come to visit her.

He was welcomed home, but after a while, the other girls left, and she stayed with her boyfriend at home. After another short time, he saw an older woman coming from the room on the right side, and the older woman greeted Vincent and looked at him strangely. He was terrified, but he calmed himself; Judith then gave the chair to the grandmother and sat down, and the conversation began.

Judith: "Kaka (old woman), this is Vincent I was telling you about" Judith used to talk to the woman about the boy she loves and told her he would visit them. "Eh, I see him; hello, boy. Is you Vincent?" Kaka asked and looked at the boy.

"Yes, Mom, Grandma too; I'm fine, and when I spoke with Judith on the phone, she told me that she had a mother; I decided to visit you, and now I come," Vincent replied with fear in his heart, but his face didn't show much.

The old woman looked at the young man without saying a word, and the young man also looked at her intermittently and looked down again; "Sweetheart (Vincent), here is Kaka I used to tell you. Do you see how young she is?" Judith interrupted with a joke because she saw that no one was talking.

As Vincent was about to answer Judith, the older woman quickly asked: "Vincent, what is your address?" is a general question that people use when talking, but the question that surprised Vincent is the second question that asks, "In what tribe are you from?"

Vincent said his home address clearly and even starts talking about how he is not used to going there because of his work, but still, he was doing it wanting to escape answering the second question Kaka asked him about the tribe. So Kaka asked again, "What tribe are you from? Answer me and proceed with your stories".

Even though Vincent didn't answer the second question, it didn't mean he didn't understand what was being asked; instead, he was thinking carefully about the best words to answer the older woman, Kaka. So when Vincent was going to speak, Judith interrupted and asked, "Kaka, why do you always bring such a question?"

But Vincent calmly said, "Judith, don't talk bad to an adult, she is a mother, and she asks a question to know my answer," Vincent said, looking at the old woman. Kaka said, "That is right; I can ask anything from anyone in my house, but I'm still waiting for you, Vincent."

"Mom, we are nothing else but Rwandans. We are RWANDANS," Vincent replied confidently but scared in the heart. Judith laughed loudly and said, "Kaka, I told you about my Vincent; pay attention to what he says and even another day (means that don't bring such questions again) to my man!" The old woman used to ask such questions to all boys that came to date, Judith.

"Vincent, you are a wise boy; Judith, give him milk; you are different from the other boys who came before you," Kaka said, and her face was very bright then, and it was apparent that she was happy. "Vincent, I can confirm you to marry my daughter now!" Kaka said it as a serious joke.

From then on, Vincent becomes friends with the whole family; he often visits the older woman whenever he has time, even if Judith was not there. The good word of unity made Kaka happy, and she became a friend of the young man.

EFFECTS OF BAD POLITICS

DIVISION AND DESCRIMINATION

After all, how we think we are different people, and that difference creates divisions. Yet, it is the beginning of knowing the value of unity because all of God's creations are useful when they are together. So we humans need to learn from the apparent difference between other living things.

Among them, one is not enough to sustain a person, but it is detrimental to us when it is taken regularly and in high quantity; yet it is only good and valuable to the human when it is compatible with others. We, humans, are so good at nature; we only differ in skin color, and so we see things. I ask myself if this could be a source of conflict and hatred that would cause us to fight each other.

You must know what is best to do at the right time and do the right thing without discrimination because God has given you what you have without discrimination. To start this, I want to go back and remind you about the following nature system of God as pre-mentioned in the previous chapter. Listen, as God set those different things to sustain humans when combined with all their other species.

Get to know that each unit of the living being you may know is not good to a person when taken alone in large quantities and often unless one combines with the other for the same benefits that complement each other to provide life. That is means that none is enough, either among us people or between people and other living organisms.

The aforementioned contains a great lesson in understanding that our differences in color, religion, place, and other differences would make us love each other and stick together. But unfortunately, distinction creates divisions, yet it is the beginning of knowing the value and importance of unity among us because all of God's creations are useful when they are together. So we humans need to learn from the obvious difference between the other living things because one is not enough to sustain a person, but it is detrimental to him, yet only when it is with others to provide life.

So we humans are so good at nature; we share everything, and we only differ in skin color and how we see things, so should this be the source of conflict and hatred to cause Racism, apartheid, and Genocide? No, it's not worth it at all, because that should make us useful because in life there are none enough alone, but to help each other and share the differences is what makes a life of peace. Each of God's creations is better together with others, creating them in different ways from other creatures to make them useful in their place; so the unity in its value joins with another to help one another to keep surviving.

Hatred, discrimination, division, and racism can all lead to serious crimes such as Genocide. It does not come as an accident but planned over a long time through strong public speaking of divisionism and dehumanization. It can come from one person or group of people or race or certain religions for their benefit, and they plan as much as possible to get them to their evil plan. A severe and cruel crime like Genocide is indeed planned and initiated by the state through public statements full of poisonous ideologies. However, if you can analyze such speeches, you can find out the reason behind them, separate yourself quickly from them or take action to stop them. Think twice and deeply interpret what you hear said by politicians and other influencers.

Remember that everything happens for a reason; what you hear and see will dictate your soul to practice it by the spirit in the body. Separatist intellectuals, for a long time, have used discriminatory language against others. Avoid listening to people like that as much as possible unless you plan to change their mindset. You need to discover the hidden motive behind what you hear or always see to prevent it from becoming a bad habit.

All about this started with hatred of specific differences, and hate can be as unexpected as it can be when someone makes you feel bad about yourself, and you feel uncomfortable. But you should not be tied to hatred for a moment longer because this ends in division and discrimination. You have to remember that time passes everything until the end of your love or affection becomes hatred, and even those who hate you will end up loving you over time; but in all things, we should not plan evil for our neighbor, always let the good come first.

Think about this scenario where a person was fighting with another using a weapon that would harm or kill a so-called powerful enemy, but as they struggle, one of them comes up with a tiny insect and gets in his eye. He is shouting, calling for help, but he is with his opponent alone on the battleground. Will his opponent not help him? If he does, will they fight again after saving each other?

What has provoked you to fight could not stop you from rescuing your friend to get the insect out of your opponent's eye. As soon as it happens, you no longer have to carry the weapons to fight again. It is a bit of intelligence to rescue your so-called enemy from such a tiny insect which is somehow impossible to kill, and again take up weapons that can cause you to kill.

At this point, I want to focus on the hatred that comes with discrimination with the intent to destroy, kill or exterminate a particular race or area inhabited by certain people. That is not a coincidence but a well-planned one that can last a lifetime. As you can see, many activities are beneficial to some, yet they are detrimental to others but have lasting results for them due to the competitive world. Therefore, I want to tell you about their preparations, the policy of discrimination through public statements; the discrimination against people keeps until it is introduced to identity cards.

The hateful public speeches favor and insult some, deprive them of humanity, and make them the core of the country's problems and injustices, so killing them is the way to solve the country's problems. All of this is perpetuated by discrimination against others and by favoring others and giving them a chance. I want to tell you that wise people have already seen what is happening.

This person can save as much as he can and separates from it. However, when there is a reason behind it, like the pursuit of benefit through looting, the so-called political interests cause many to engage in Genocide, and relief and saving efforts are lost.

Avoid all forms of hate, carefully analyze every speech you hear that leads to division and be able to identify the reason behind it and act quickly because you already know what will happen. So don't blindly accept everything you've heard. Be cautious.

CONFLICTS AND WARS

In any case, the cause of the conflict will not prevent you from helping your neighbor to remove the small insect that has gone into his eye, and as soon as it is over, you will no longer lift the weapon to fight again. After all, it is not wise to help to remove a tiny insect that cannot kill fresh and get up again with weapons that can kill your partner.

The above idea will help you to avoid making hasty decisions, which will help you to make fair judgments when you see or recover from a conflict. It seems to be everyday life, people become friends, and it is common to see misunderstandings among them. It's just that for the sake of politics where things change, and you discover that your loved ones have become your enemies by tomorrow. For some people, you know they hate each other, but you find them talking like lovers, and they laugh a lot, maybe because they reconciled or ignored something, betraying, or for the sake of politics.

In life, there are friends of faith, and I can call these loyal friends. These are always with you; whether you are sad or happy, you will always see them by your side. When you feel sad, those friends will comfort you. When you hurt, they heal you. They give you the hands and shoulders to walk with if you stumble. They will correct your mistakes politely, and they will not go away. The Bible goes on to say that those friends are better than brothers and sisters. Some friends can confuse you with trustworthiness, but they are following and attached to the benefits they see in you. They are there when they see you in the wanted benefits, stay close to you, and in your happiness. And even in the sadness, they are there too; sadly, they will leave you when you no longer deliver the benefits because they find someone else to help them.

It is regrettable to hear about people who fell in love with each other or friendly countries that are now separated and are no longer in friendship. Each side seeks to inflict dishonesty and ridicule on the other with the secrets they once knew. The secrets you always hear have a reason.

I led the association of students studying clinical medicine in Rwanda for two years. Experience is not measured by the years a person lived or the years spent in something like leading or managing a certain group of people but based on the lesson someone has learned. The clinical Officers program, also known as Physician Assistant Program in Rwanda, was a new University program with its own set of challenges to reach the level of other countries in which it is located. It had problems compared to other University health-related programs, and some time ago, it did not appear on the job list as the new emerging profession.

It all started with a friend we talked to all the time, and he came up with a way to campaign for me to lead the forum of its students because he felt that I could only do what he thought. He would think that I would implement what he thought. But in leadership, you make the right decision in favor of the benefits for the majority! He felt he would play a vital role in the decision-making process; He wanted me to ignore other members, including those who worked with me and other institutions at the University and outside of it. So me and him, it's a two-person decision.

This entire he thought of before he even planned it, and when I got to leadership, I started working with anyone who had an idea, and all made the decisions for us with no one in mind. It surprised me that when I began to see some old letters I didn't know, they seemed to be waiting for me to sign them. I started to see that some of the comments were disrespectful because they didn't fit in with what was planned. His team wanted to ignore the others' ideas even though they were understandable, but if they didn't fit in with a pre-set plan, it meant any argument was unconvincing, and I had no reason to comment. I noticed that there are sections. One section that feels it understood the vision of the association; and is the one that has brought about a revolution. It is also the part that better organizes the election that puts me in charge of their plans rather than being a leader for all members. Another section wants to know the information better; the achievement will depend on what we have decided together.

We used to have meetings full of mismatching and misunderstanding; many usually left the meeting with a headache, what a moment! I meet a serious challenge of division. It was clear that we needed to have the same information, we had a lot of meetings to share the information with reliable evidence, and we could figure out where to start. In a few days, all the leaders and members knew what we had, what we were missing, and how we would get the solutions. I had a lot of information from both sides, and we started to make joint decisions because I already knew the true mission of a good leader. I also found out why the other person advertised me. I remind you that there is no difference between people, only how they feel and respect their responsibilities; this makes some to be heroes and make some to be cowards.

Of course, I started having problems with him in a way that I didn't know, and he and his group started arguing that I wasn't going to follow their plans, that I was killing things, and that I could have left the office without a second chance. It was hard to do what they wanted one hundred percent. Things have grown so slowly that there has been a lot of contempt and desire, and they are trying to take over the leadership.

He concluded that the best way was to see the leader leave and make it clear that he wanted to replace me with the help of some of his listeners. After all, where there are problems, everyone has their way of thinking and a way of solving those problems. But when there is a disagreement, one no longer wants to share the way of solving the issue but wants to use his means against the authorities. However, it all has a reason behind it. We met in so many ways that it (the association) seemed to be led by two leaders. Here, it was still very easy because he had a colleague who was in charge of law and discipline in the committee, who was always his defender but instead blamed the rest of the administration, including me.

Things continued to get worse until the president of the general association was suspended and reinstated by other senior executives in collaboration with members who refused to disrespect him. After all, the problems in the journey should not make the traveler forget the purpose of travel. It is essential always to be responsible for all the struggles and keep the promises you have made. Of course, it took a lot of effort to get things back on track so that I could end the conflict that started to grow. The members who thought and looked closely saw that slow progress came from two people who failed to reconcile. He tried to use some of the leaders; many fell into wrongdoing and were punished by law until, even more, we penalized the other law enforcement officials.

My direct opponent has never been punished, and he was the source of the mistakes others have made. The people who were friends to him were the ones he used to break the law, yet he left with holy hands. He used people to achieve his goals. That is also politics, where the intelligent people use the rest to accomplish oneness responsibilities. It soon became apparent that it was difficult for him to work with the administration, which led to the fact that he still had a problem with the association's president.

In leadership, you may disagree with the leader, but it should not override the leader's responsibility for the benefit of the rest. When you want to know the root causes of the problem, it requires you to dig deep and have enough information to help you make the right decision that will help in resolving the conflict. We've had a lot of meetings that keep me from agreeing with each other because open-ended discussions are the answer. It is not surprising to see two opposing sides meeting peacefully in a place where they have prepared themselves, and no one else knows. It's fantastic to see them laugh, hug, and even conversation; each side knows their strengths or weaknesses.

In any case, political conflict should not prevent one from living everyday life nor allow one to think of harming another. We laughed, and he told me what he wanted me to help him with, and I told him how I could help him regardless of the opinions of others. When he saw that it didn't get to his point, the conversations would change, and we would come back without a definite conclusion.

I want to tell you that success does not come from words but from serving, and it is the key to lasting success; what we do for people will also dictate what they do for us; which is why they continue to trust us to continue to help them in the position we have. Therefore, stop wasting your time planning the path you will take to achieve success but do your daily work leading to your goals. If you do this sincerely, you will earn a great victory, which is God's plan for your life.

As you have already seen in the story above, I hope you see that when it comes to leadership or other interests, especially those of politics, the relationship may end, but the responsibility has to be fulfilled. Surely in any circumstance, stick to your commitment to achieving your goal without harming anyone. Otherwise, the wars will not end, and the love will not end; this is why you should do well in everything. As you try to restore peace, you agree to accept all feelings of hatred, go beyond them, and seek conversations that bring each one back to the line of stability. You have to do this to know the real reason behind the conflict.

It seems normal that when someone loves you so much, they are only left with the time to hate you and vice versa because everything is controlled by the time God has set. Of course, this should not change our daily lives; what is happening to you now and tomorrow would change and tell a different story. After all, we live in a time, and God controls time. You don't have to beg people to love you; it doesn't matter if your neighbors hate you. If you know what to do, do it for peace and prosperity. Doing so will make your share and contribution more complete as time goes on and on. That means as we keep being alive in the world for a long time, the opposing sides will reconcile, and long-term friends can separate, but in all, there is nothing to stop the life of one of us.

There is much of what we go through in our relationships. Some things keep a good relationship and unite us, but there are many to separate us. In life, some endure us and find that they did not only come to be our friends but came with a purpose. There are many reasons to unite us, but some ignore them because of the many benefits we can gain from creating conflict.

Struggling for power is one of the leading causes of war. Due to this, a leader can do everything possible to sit in the leadership without apparent reason. They fight to get the honor and delight of giving orders and being respected by doing what the leader says. You will also find that a person who comes to power has used all possible means, tricks, and conspiracies to get to the desired position. Whatever method he used, whatever the cost would cost him, whether war, betrayal, or murder, the person would do it to achieve the goal. This one does not care about the wounds left behind; the goal is to achieve the glory that comes from a good leadership position. The interests and privileges that some people want by seeking fame, respect, wealth accumulation, favor, dictatorship, nepotism, division and discrimination, injustice, the killing of opponents, corruption, and domination, are some of the things causing war in a given country or a given continent.

At this point, the International community should no longer ignore the looting of natural resources and the plots of serious theft of natural resources such as minerals and oils in a specific country. That may lead to political tensions, with some defending their Countries and others accusing others of robbery and theft, turning them into poverty and wealth, respectively. Here, it has led to division in the people with some supporting the other side, terrorist groups escalating and insecurity leaving people dead. Others become refugees in their own countries or cross borders. The situation is even worse, as other countries begin to wrongly interfere in the politics of other countries, often in the interests of politics as well. It is usually highly likely that the country may need the help of other countries to restore peace and security.

There is always an explanation of the terms of the restoring peace agreement, but there may be another attached mission. If it has, it does not appear in the official documents; it only remains in the minds of the people or the country that drafted it well. It is a long-term mission which is why some tasks have failed to be completed, but the messengers have yet to return because the reason behind the mission was unsuccessful.

In this case, the war lasts for a long time, the conflict takes over, and the people lose their property and even their lives. Yet, the nations are united, new politics are initiated, and the international community stands up. Still, they have differing views on one plan to save such a war-torn country for other unknown missions hiding behind reality. You will often find that the failure to complete the task is not due to limited ability; all the effort and calculations go to the other reason behind the scenes. It is time for real humanitarian and charitable projects to be introduced. It is good to be involved in solving the real problem to save the life of humankind. Where possible, with mutual relationship, you will discuss other interests after restoring peace and security in a particular country because political interests are also needed".

The people's poverty can also cause wars due to the wrong policies of the looters who do not show the strength and practical projects to advance the country, only for themselves. When that happens, tensions rise, the people fearlessly oppose the government for change, and the evil government confronts the people out of fear and resentment of change. When you get to the point where you have the people's trust, you do not commit atrocities, you do not kill people, and you do not commit treason; instead, you do your duty as best you can. That allows them to see none else to replace you, and even if it is the right time to leave, you say goodbye and thank God for helping you in your responsibility. You also have to thank those who trusted you and gave you responsibility. Just leave peace and security, stay in your country and reap the seeds you sow while you are still a leader. The people will say goodbye to you and remain proud of your deeds. Here, it is also Democracy.

Wars are some of the things prepared intelligently, and it is too sad to find some that have been planned and anticipated before the people who will die as sacrifices for the war planner's achievements. War may be the final solution and the resolution to something bad that needs to be handled; understandably, the battle may be the last option. Here, I want to return to those innocent people who lost their lives because of the fight planned by people who want to gain power, take revenge, and gain access to some golden resources and respect for winning high office.

Those people don't even care about the things that will be destroyed; they push many people into the war, including unprofessional people like children who usually and typically need to be protected. Surprisingly, you may find some people engaged in war and strike without an apparent reason for them to engage in war. Remember that war is to destroy, not build, and so only follow people who you know one's clear and clean vision and missions. They may have some masks; I need you to think twice and live in the future today. Don't go blind in war without a clear reason unless you find it the final option after failing the rest of the diplomatic sessions to save and protect the world.

POLITICAL TOOLS AND THEIR IMPACTS

INTERNATIONAL RELATIONSHIP

Keep and control your relationships with others and know for sure that you should treat them well at all costs. Remember to be humble as the cost of shared development by people for your love and kindness to them, for they will always unite not to fight but to pull you up and fight against your temporary enemies.

At this point, I return to the relationship and partnership that unites people, countries, and continents. Let's look at the real reasons for the association; and why aid is being provided to a particular country or continent. You will often find political interests in a specific country as the real reason for assistance in other countries in development, security, and governance.

Love is an essential element in human life characterized by various emotions that have a lot of meaning and a lot to hide. Some people associate because of secrets, so it becomes the norm because of the benefits of their relationship.

Life consists of helping each other, supporting each other, and so on, and this often happens to people with good relationships as countries do. Borrowing, helping, and cooperating remain the common goal. A good relationship is the main reason for cooperation. In this world, none loves you more than you love yourself, and no country loves any country more for its development than for itself. Remember that Jesus also asked you to love your neighbor as you love yourself, which means that even the one who tried to love you would love you as much as he loves himself, win and win situation.

We see a lot of help and support as a sign of a good relationship but have many reasons behind it. That has happened to some people, even to the relations of nations and continents. Being able to accurately analyze each situation to determine the cause of action is a method that should be used in every area of life and relationships between us. We need to know why we are so symbiotic. Undoubtedly, people, we should live in peace and love. At this point, a person should be ready to make the same sacrifices to show love to each other. This is not necessarily impossible, but we have to try to do it at any reasonable cost. It also requires us to develop a sense of love to understand why people can love each other because it often coincides with what they know as secrets and goals about each other.

Explaining exactly how people need each other requires careful consideration of how a tiny insect or small particle goes into a person's eyes. Still, it prevents a person from being able to do anything (blindness for short while). It requires a person to get close to an opponent, even in a conflict. They must put aside their war to save the opponent's life. Will they resume the fight and continue the fighting? To the best of our ability, conflicts should not arise between us; as Jacob, chapter 4, verse 1 asks, "Where do quarrels and wars come from? "It shows us that wars always come out of the evil we enjoy that keeps fighting in our souls.

If wars arise between us, it results from the enjoyment of evil that fights within us. So don't ignore your partner, refusing to save that tiny insect from his eye; even if the person is your enemy, you should help him. And just as with the help of a little problem, let them teach you a lesson and turn to the big issue in your midst, then get rid of it because it is more harmful than the other small insects that made you reconcile for a while.

It is regrettable and likely that there may be another part apart from opponents enjoying the battle. And the one who will be enjoying the results of the fights. I also want to talk about those who create a deliberate struggle to gain their income and then mislead the rest. Think twice and deepest before you make every decision.

Just as none is rich enough to live in wealth without the support of others, any country cannot live well without good relations with other countries; even if not all countries, it is worthy of having good relations with other countries. Remember that no country has compassion for another country other than its political interests. Nowadays, everything has become a competition; we are still in the image of imperialism. We are in such a time of great inequality that understanding requires me to use examples as if one country or some countries has/have surpassed the rest of the continent.

I hope you have heard of the meetings organized by one country and with the continent. You will hear that they will hold a China-Africa summit, a Russia-Africa summit, a Germany-Africa summit and a US-EU summit, the Africa-France Summit, and many more. Some of which seem to be nations' competitions on the same continent. There is also a hidden reason behind those meetings, and if you think about it, you can see the real reason why each speech spoken in it may have a long-term effect. The competition in partnership with the continent should be for the benefit of both parties. If the country helps you economically, it must be a win-and-win system.

You will hear one saying, "I will help in establishing good political principles," and another saying, "we will work together in military cooperation." Another say, "I will not interfere in politics; I will work with you only on economic issues." These partnerships are great and are needed, but the benefits should be comparable to the impact, and the partner's options should determine this. Sometimes the help determines the behavior, and the use of the aid provided, all in a way that will bring benefits to the donor country. Unfortunately, you will also find that loans provided will turn into long-term debt, close to capturing and owning the land.

You will hear someone else say that "I will help them in everything to reach the international level. I will teach them how good governance is, and democracy will be strengthened"". In any case, the partnership always has a valid reason for its Immediate and long-term interests. That is why thinking about the real reasons behind the cooperation shown by some of these countries, would help in making good decisions for the benefit of the people. It doesn't seem easy to decide who to work with and who will take us to our destination. It means that the donor country should also consider the goals of the receiver countries, which determine the relationship with other continents or countries. The combined output should aim for equal benefits on both sides.

We should always analyze why each partnership is required; there should be an agreement on the benefits to both parties and the guidelines that will be followed to avoid interfering in non-contractual matters. Cooperation exists because each country seeks the betterment of its people more than the people of other countries. However, countries may think, and work together about a better future in the region, their continent, and the world at large.

POLITICAL AIDS AND FINANCIAL SUPPORT

President Paul KAGAME once said, "Aids is more political than anything else, Markets are less political, and markets are neutral." He said this at the East African Capital Markets Conference held in Kigali- on 12 February 2015.

Undoubtedly the support from relations of certain countries or among countries with international or private organizations; reflects a good and strong relationship between them through development efforts or economic integration. Indeed it is an economic partnership that leads to development, yet this is politically complex. It can reach an extent they can use it to support the rebels or any other terrorist group that seeks to overthrow the government or create insecurity in the country for some gain; surprisingly, most of the profits go to its supporters.

Competition for aid continues to the point where other countries have come up with different but more insecure aid inside the country. Some support the current government, others help the coup attempt, like the war of other nations inside the country, and the citizens face endless danger. That is easy to explain to a person who wants a positive change, but it is also difficult to tell a person or a government that is always in the mood for help and has firm debts that are hard to repay.

I was born shortly after the 1994 Genocide against the Tutsi; a clear history shows that the country was grieving the loss of parents, friends, and relatives. The government has left with survivors with disabilities; others are full of wounds and the deep grief of losing their loved ones. The country was also full of orphans left behind after the loss of their families. In addition, the country lost a lot of intellectuals and workers, and there is a lot of grief and sorrow. When efforts were being made to unite and rebuild the country, there was a need for capable leadership with a living purpose to bring the country back to life.

Of course, there was a need for more friends from neighboring and far-flung countries and individuals to help the country as much as possible and get things back on track. We are thankful that funding has been provided in many ways to rebuild the country and preserve political interests. However, It is sad to see the support given to the people who want to bring the country back into the darkness. Some can provide funding for security breaches for the purpose and benefit of providing it, so be wise. I grew up hearing parents appreciate the foreign support provided to the country; some of the help came from food. I vividly remember a white center close to our home offering food such as edible oils, peas, blends, and more.

The center was very popular with the community, and the local management (Rwandans) of the center felt great because it was not easy for the child to study there. People at that time were accustomed to aid rather than finding solutions independently. It seemed like a familiar proverb: "giving someone a fish and not teaching them how to fish." Imagine getting food, but don't worry about how long it will take if you continue to receive support.

Why not help modernize agriculture and get enough of that food, and take it to market? Sometimes, some form of aid can make people lazy. Think about why the support you will receive will help you to know that you will not always receive it and start to think about your future in its absence.

The time has come, and such aids stopped. The government has taken all steps to cope with this, as a nursing woman does to take off the baby from breastfeeding (weaning process). However, it was difficult for some stuck in that lousy dependence behavior. Some say they are not happy with the government measure and tell others that "you will see"; this government will starve us.

Surprisingly, for the next two years, they changed their minds and started looking for answers until they changed their behaviors and started working on their development. Some decisions seem wrong, but they have long-term benefits for the people. That should help you understand the strategies of the healthy government and other international agencies that look to the better future of our world, such as the; UN, WHO, UNESCO, and many others that are not biased towards the lasting interests of just one country.

We heard that there are many benefits to the giver; keep in mind that the hand of giving is more blessed than the hand of receiving, as the word of God shows. There is help coming in without asking. So the person who gives you the support thinks about it in your absence and, for some reason, surprises you with assistance. It is good but be careful because the donor can also decide how and what you will use to match the reason for giving it to you. The donor often has vested interests; if he has been taught by theology, he seeks to please God to be just and to have a good heart. But if you don't think so, it is for some reason; if you are wise enough, this will help you decide whether to accept it.

There is also the need for support from an individual or a country. Here a country has to sit on a budget and find a loophole where they need help from a person or government with a good relationship.

The donor thinks about it and looks at your relationship and interest in it to the extent that it can depend on how you will use it. This ensures that what you want and how you use it will be consistent with what the donor wants. The difference deduction of the payment period and the use of the loan all have reasons behind it. Many countries are embedded in debt that is not easy to pay back.

The above has the effect of being taken over by another country to the point where they dictate what you should or not do. Is there any country being pitied by another country? Sometimes, the misuse of the loan that has been demanded may be due to looting and poorly planned projects.

There is a need to change the process of applying for a loan without reason and the actual projects that will consume the loan; this will have a positive effect by not going into long-term debt and being unable to repay it. There is a reason behind lending, funding, and their use. And when it comes to international relations, it is more political than most think.

TECHNOLOGY AND SCIENCES IN POLITICS

As human beings, we are products of what we often hear or see, which determines our behavior as politically motivated through the media and modern technology. Therefore, the level and the use of technology and media; clearly define the life of a particular country.

Let me start by telling you how technology can make us rich or poor, live longer, or shorten our lives. It makes us smarter, puts our minds back, keeps our culture, or destroys it. It allows us to build or destroy a country, makes us believe or destroy our beliefs, and enables us to expand and strengthen our friendship or destroy it. It even makes us choose.

Technology is the development of a particular person, region, country, or continent. Someone who doesn't have or know how to use technology seems to be hidden from information, or his knowledge is limited. Conversely, a person or country without technology appears to remain in the darkness and permanently locked in an underdeveloped mind.

Technology has replaced natural functionality, the same as modernization. Therefore, there is no choice but to leave traditionally to embrace technology and know-how and use it well in our daily lives because it seems that we become more productive as we use technology.

Here I will use real-life examples of the differences between people and countries that also come from differences in the use of technology. For instance, it took Bezos's technology to set up an online shopping site AMAZON and connect it with buyers worldwide. It prompted Bill Gates to think about technology and launch a project that brought Microsoft.

It also required Steve Jobs to think about Apple's technology, which made him rich in his time. Bill Gates and Steve Jobs became rich when we bought Microsoft in our Apple computers and other similar products. Bezos has approached us with a wide range of products on the big website of AMAZON.

The same thing happened with Mark Zuckerberg; when he found out that we needed information and to connect on our computers and phones, he brought us Facebook, WhatsApp, and other social media. We had no other choice except to follow him and enrich him. What happened to Google and other social networking sites that made the owners rich? We also have different benefits, depending on how we use them. The secret is to know how to use technology.

Starting a business that doesn't think about technology is a loss; it is just a local development that you don't benefit from elsewhere. Intelligent business people think about technology and make a lot of money from it, even though we can use it to do bad things like stealing and destroying people and things. Technology requires you to think about and analyze every one of the technologies you use, especially what you see or hear on social media. On the other hand, some people have seen technology, especially social media, as a form of entertainment; this makes them stop their work to have fun that can last for a short time but have a negative and lasting effect.

There is no doubt that what we see, hear, and use technology has a different mission and purpose and has a positive or detrimental effect on the health of those who will use it; beware of technology. It is not surprising to hear that someone wants to buy a good phone, and its quality is based on its excellent photography skills. The users immediately think of sharing photos with friends and videos that look good using Facebook, Instagram, WhatsApp, TikTok, Twitter, and other fast-paced social media.

It's better to send and share photos on social media (although there are also reasons behind it, depending on the person who did it and the recipient). Still, some seem to be blinded to other important uses of computers or phones rather than taking pictures, watching, and calling.

Remember, some social media sites are not limited to sending photos, calling, and texting for fun but also for building a nation, knowing and sharing useful information, being a good businessman using social media, and promoting and helping other users. We will continue to need technology as the days go by; remembering the days of COVID-19 when either paying your bills or importing them through technology has increased dramatically. In addition to helping you avoid COVID-19, it has been shown that technology was used to accelerate excellent service.

Remember that technology is evolving every day, so start not only from what you see but also from discovering your own for your own and your country's development. Otherwise, you will be a slave to technology, and it may even harm you, making you poor instead of promoting you.

Let me take another example that highlights the significant differences between countries in terms of knowledge and the use of technology. Technology has made some countries the most competitive, and technology has made countries achieve great human achievements, such as stepping on the Moon. But on the other hand, technology has boosted some countries' economies and created a huge gap between other countries.

We cannot ignore the fact that it has allowed countries to acquire powerful and destructive weapons for their safety. With that being said, you can immediately think of the United States as the seat and the definition of productive technology. You may have thought of China, which seems to have decided to use technology in economically viable projects, even though they have not given up on using it in other ways as security.

You may have thought of the USA, China, Russia, and many other European countries because of the sun of technology that seems to be shining on them. It is evident that when a country can effectively manage its citizens through the use of technology in the development of the country, such a country will bring different regionally and internationally. Simply it is necessary to manage the use of technology. Only in this case, there is control over another country's technology and its benefits to the extent that you can find citizens who behave like they are in any other country. Surprizingly, you may find some have more information in another country, follow their plans, and always dream of going to that country, feeling that they will change their life there; this is the product of managing technology. Recognize that technology and the media are the most political tools.

Technology has now reached a point where I still need to learn, and there are still many important things to do in its projects. Technology is a required tool and mandatory law for everyone to use daily. It is necessary for countries in their governance, security, and development. Technology is in all sectors of life and is being used in various ways for its own sake and mission.

As you read this book, technology has played a significant role, and I am grateful to those who have contributed to its (technology) development. You've seen a lot of people in the same place who are so busy connected to the internet with computers or smartphones that it's hard to find someone to converse with. However, if you ask them what they are doing with those technological tools, they can reply with the different things that match their interest.

There is a compelling reason for someone to use technology. Some use technology to their advantage; others use it to their detriment. Technology can help you to be better or make you worse, technology helps some to thrive and others to make them very poor, yet you find it has something to do with the development of someone else who has been able to control it. The blessed country is one with people who use technology wisely to create and innovate something for their development.

Thinking about the use of technology and what you intend to hear or see in the media through social media helps you to know the benefits of what you follow and the reasons behind it all. What I have said above shows that politics is in our lives or daily lives, which is why there is no organization which does not use politics; it can also be good or bad depending on how it is used or received by the people. This has changed the course of our lives so much that our lives have changed due to politics. All of life has been political.

The media has been a channel through which the government conveys policies to the people. It has been a critical partner in making the public aware of what the government thinks and helping the people convey their views to the national administration. Effective media does not work in a one-on-one way for some benefit; instead, it should connect the government with the people, inform the public of government policies, and provide feedback to people on government policies. Dissemination of information and being a trusted public speaker or representative are the responsibilities of the media.

What I am saying above is the actual responsibility of the media, both for the state and the people. It all changes when other benefits emerge, resulting in fabricated stories and rumors, and the reality is lost. Some states have publicly violated the freedom of the press, and the media and journalists have been shut down for publishing stories. However, we cannot ignore the fact that some wrongly use and hide behind Democracy to fabricate stories that undermine the current administration for the benefit of third parties.

Good policy determines what the media should give to people for a better life, to live in peace and security, and to encourage the people to achieve these by participating. Suppose a journalist needs to collect news from you and analyze it thoroughly to find out the purpose of the story you are providing. This will help you to know the story of the right publication for people to thrive and be at peace. You don't have to be pushed by money or bribes to publish information that causes war or conflict in a country or region. It would help if you did not divulge what you see in the interest you want, regardless of its impact on other people.

We must know that every published story has a purpose, and all good and evil can be objective. Be aware that some rumors and stories tell the truth, and some take the true story and add something to it for a certain purpose. We also note that there are reports intended to be of personal benefit to the publisher and stories intended to benefit the public at large or collectively.

The media is the mainstay of significant powers in disseminating political principles in other countries. In this regard, the countries should not disclose the information and what should be kept confidential have to stay in the country. The media has removed colonialism from any physical integration in other countries. Still, the media and technology are bringing a new way of determining governance in other countries without requiring them to go there physically.

Another country's media may provoke people to bring political change to their country. After staring at others' lifestyles and seeing their freedom, they may immediately decide to fight for their rights in their country of origin and for release from what they do that is not legal until it is legal. Sometimes we need to analyze what we see more profoundly, and then we do not rush to destroy what was built. The rest is straightforward to bring about change due to the media. Nowadays, when there are no media, there is no change too.

POLITICS AND CONSIPIRACY

Remember that betrayal is based on a lot of information displayed or shared with others; a betrayal appears where there is a relationship, this requires the traitor to have all the information on the other side. Secrets make a person to differ from each other in performance and behavior. It distinguishes individuals or countries in many ways, including the economy.

One has a secret that helps in the protection of wealth. That means knowing the secret I use; you can be like me or destroy any of my achievements. Ask yourself if any country knows the secret the USA uses to build and protect the country at all levels to remain a world power. Undoubtedly, that country would be as strong as the USA after implementing that secret.

Secrecy has become a secret and countries or peoples are aligned with secrets; it is difficult to find them in conflict because unity protects what one has or knows from one another. Have you understood the agreement that countries with nuclear weapons have in common? They should negotiate and prevent other nations from making atomic weapons. Is this done to protect the world? Or it is to protect the secret of making the weapon.

If a certain country uses a secret to have a strong military that is much protected and you do not think it is easy to be revealed unless there is a spy who can uncover and breaks the secret. Suppose there is a secret that makes a country economically secure, which is protected by national competition for development.

Thinking and discovering your secret but using or collaborating with others to implement it will make that secret a lasting success as long as you keep it. Remember that there is a mutually beneficial partnership, but no country thinks for the best of the other countries than itself; believe it or not, when that happens, you're colonized. There are also political interests as reasons that are behind the relations of certain countries.

Betrayal is not a word that has come up quickly as that without purpose and that is why Judas betrayed Jesus for his benefit. Remember Judas was one of his disciples, who lived with him daily, heard him saying good, acting skillfully, and listening to his authority. Jesus trusted Judas as his apostle, and Judas believed Jesus was his master. No one else would betray Jesus without coming out from his disciples, who used to discuss everything with him, so no one but only the disciples because no one else would know Jesus very well than them. So there is a reason behind Judas' act of Kissing Jesus alone; it was like a great act of love for him but hid betrayal. It is difficult to imagine how he did it as a sign of Jesus' presence in others. It's an act of love that was hiding treason.

I also want to return to the point that espionage and betrayal are not just acts of the current moment. Do you remember the story of Samson and his wife, Delilah? And this confirms that the enemy may not be far from your house. That was a girl sent by her nation to discover the secret that made Samson so powerful. Delilah fell in love with a purpose for the whole country; she had to show the love that would make Samson break a secret that seemed to betray him.

Of course, if Delilah had achieved what she wanted early on, she would not have become a woman of Samson. Samson did everything for his wife as a man on duty so that he would make the woman change her heart and be faithful. Remember that while they were walking, they met a lion; Samson fought it until he killed it. He does all this to show the woman that he is responsible for protecting the family.

They say that "A dead ear doesn't hear" Rwandan proverb. Samson has seen a lot as a sign that the woman may have had a reason to bring him in love and that the mission was about to kill him, but he continues to play until he breaks the secret. Let me tell you he thought he has with a trusted wife; kindly stop playing with the secret you see in your family and your country at large because you may find yourself disclosing it to the enemy.

Samson finally broke the secret, "Since I was born, I had never shaved, which means if I shaved my hair, there was no power in me." But unfortunately, the man fell asleep, the woman shaved him, and as soon as the

Philistines (their enemies) arrived, they found him and tied him up; Samson ended up dead.

Let me give you another example that allows you to take care of yourself and control the reasons behind the good that you see as not being hiding treachery or a lie intended to rob you, just as Jacob did to deceive Esau with his blessing. Remember that he gave him a delightful red meal but a very meal; Esau agreed to exchange it with his legacy to Jacob, his brother. His hunger would not kill him, but he decided to trade his blessing from his father, for he was the heir of the eldest son.

Maybe Esau was playing with the brother so that the brother would not betray him, that his father would not obey him, and even felt that God would not do it. As a reminder, God is constantly keeping track of our promises and watching over how we will fulfill the contracts, so don't play with promises you won't keep. For God is a God that promises and will meet all commitments. Jacob was blessed with Esau as promised. For Christians, the history of Esau affected him and his descendants. It is a pity that a brother would be jealous of you and take you away from yours regardless of being of the same blood. There is a reason behind everything;

even if it is right in your eyes, it can negatively affect you.

As you read this book, you may have thought of many other examples of serious betrayals that have led to conflicts and wars that I have never written about before. As I said above, it requires a traitor to have enough information. Instead, the traitor always comes out surprisingly, he turns out because of what you told him, and he betrays you for some reason. The consequences can be positive or negative when confidential information is leaked, depending on the source. In the country, when someone broke secrets, they called him a traitor, but when he discovered some secrets, they called him a spy. As a reminder, information, conversations, and more, we always talk to close friends; in the end, you may find everything goes public. That shows that no one is trustworthy. So I urge you to be cautious about what to say to anyone because they have a different reason to behave differently than friendship. Here, it is not to say that you should always be suspicious but to remind you that too much faith can end in betrayal and that a believer in the Son of Man will be cursed.

You will see that many have achieved a lot, and others have maintained what they have through treachery. At every step they take, they hurt many, crucifying others to the point of shedding innocent blood. Of course, you can be an excellent public speaker, but to be honest, people like them know how to speak nicely to win people's trust. The difference is that they will not be implemented because a lot of their energy stays in planning how they will use that power again to get to the next level. Action is better than words.

INTEGRATION OF RELIGION IN POLITICS

This is a concept that has been in place for a long time, but it has become a great deal to bring about the establishment of the monarchy and overthrow the rest. Religion also has been a primary weapon of colonialism and nationalism. Many were killed for their disrespect for this doctrine and others for their religious beliefs.

Religions have taken such a step that in any country in the world, you will find a certain belief in it. We must believe that God is always present in our daily work. This happens to the point that even murderous activity in so-called God's name seems to be fighting for God. Nowadays, there is no country in the world without a particular religion; some have dominant religion, and some countries are like sharing believers among different churches.

Here if you want, you can call it democracy and everyone's freedom by going to a particular religion, which is pretty perfect. Religion has established many leaders and overthrown monarchs and other dominant leaders we have ever known. So it is no wonder that a particular country is based on certain beliefs so that all decisions taken are as relevant to the majority of believers of a specific religion in the special nation.

It is not surprising to see a particular religion rebelling or supporting the protests. Religions have such a strong power that the Pope is among the most outstanding leaders worldwide without hesitation. There is none to deny this because many countries must implement his decisions, and where it is not respected, it is a rebellion against the Pope and the Catholic in general.

Without action, in some places, the Christians and Muslims may keep into a quarrel. It is also challenging to find a compromise between the Protestants and their derivatives churches with the Catholics, one of which has its truth and will continue to do so until one fails and give up. Keep in mind that the people will keep their principles, regulations, and doctrines until they get disappointed.

Unfortunately, there are Christians who argue with other Christians from different churches. These may come from the minor changes that came from conflicts between religious leaders but bring battles within people to the point of undermining one's faith. For example, many of us know the two types of Islam, the Sunnis, and the Shias. Both are Islam members, but there is a difference between them because Shiites believe son in low of Mohamed, Ali, while the Sunnis believe that the redemption of people will depend on how one believes in Allah, His prophets, and believe Muhammad as the great prophet. From that difference is where the quarrel arises between them. Often you will find it contrary to the Quran and what the Prophet of God, Mohamed (May God grant him peace and blessings), asks.

Religion has already wrongly convinced us that it is normal for citizens to compete and fight because of their different beliefs. It means that Christians can fight Muslims to the point of committing crimes, mainly in civil war, and the international communities are ready to come to the rescue as peacekeepers. That can happen in the interior, and conflicts arise among the people because of religion. Remember the civil war in MALI called Islamist Tuareg Rebellion since 2012, The Boko Haram uprising in Nigeria, and the conflict with the Al-Shabaab militia in Somalia.

You may immediately remember or think of some countries that have reached the peak of religious conflict. I want to remind you of the conflicts and religious wars such as the Crusades, which began in 1095 and were fought by Latinos who wanted to liberate the catholic holy land from Islamic rule. In the war, the Pope blessed the soldiers to fight for God and opened Heaven's gates for those who would be killed in battle because "God wills it."

Remember, too, the hatred of the Nazis against the Jews that led to genocide against Jews; it was racist hatred, but the other reason was historically rooted in European Christians who hated Jews for a long. Let me also remind you of the conflict between the Catholic Church and the Protestants in the 16th century. It was after the founding of Protestants in 1515 after the revolt against catholic rule in many European countries.

Let me continue to share that history and talk about the conflict in the Central African Republicans, where members of the Christian faith have fought fiercely against Muslims in an open civil war until the international communities and countries stood up for help. I am sure that you know many religious terrorist groups that are determined to fight for the sovereignty of their religion to the extent that they want the laws of their faith to be respected throughout the country.

Boko haram, Al-Qaeda, Al-Shabaab, the Christian Anti-balaka coalition, and other religious-based terrorist groups have been formed because of religious interference in politics. Undoubtedly, many countries and international organizations have taken a stand against these terrorist groups to restore good relations with the people without compromising the member of the faith, based on the principles of democracy that we believe in when it is well used, not as a pretense.

It is regrettable to see religion as we already know it, and then there are conflicts. I always wonder if the answer is in faith because if religion had a solution, we would not see people of the same religion arguing. Please think of the Christians themselves by name, the Seventh-day Adventists and Islam, who ended up being divided into factions that could lead to misunderstandings and result in long-term conflict.

Some Protestants disagree with Catholics, Adventists disagree with Reformers, and it is well-known that Sunnis disagree with Shiites. It is common to find that a particular terrorist group is sponsored or supported by the government or other countries in a way that they accept or deny. Such assistance intends for many other political and economic purposes or the dissemination of governance systems such as democracy, communism, or the domination of monopoly governance systems.

Religion has ended many lives; sacrificing themselves and killing others may be because their beliefs are not in line with the politics of their own countries. From ancient times before Jesus, people were murdered and persecuted for their beliefs. However, this did not leave the time of Jesus because He was a great example of enduring suffering as He is God's sacrifice to save human beings; this was not unjust suffering for Christian believers because, for Jesus, it was as crucial as many beliefs.

Since then, the persecution and death of many for their faith have not stopped. Even murders like these appeared in Madagascar, Uganda, Sweden, Japan, and many more. There is even a place where a particular religious member cannot go to live in peace because their behavior is completely based on their religious beliefs, which are different from the habitant's beliefs.

It is only because some people want to fight for a particular religion and have a lot to gain as the founders or leaders, which makes them want to use every possible means to keep the faith alive by deceiving many.

I firmly believe that religion should have brought us together in love, just as God is love. Still, the wealth or interests that follow the founders of a particular religion and the spreading of its members lead to wars and conflicts through competition and conflict. We all know that when the contest is over, there is a lot of damage.

It's just that these things go beyond war or conflict and come in a beautiful and convincing Image. And that's because many of us love the good and find ourselves solving and fulfilling the desires of the one who came and founded a particular religion or brought a specific belief. Yet, our wealth has been taken away, and we remain in poverty.

CONCLUSION

It's great that you've reached the end of this book; I'm glad you're going to use the lessons you've learned to change your community. Now you know that all good and evil things are politically motivated, and Religion is politically motivated. You will hear some religious believers believe that they have nothing to do with politics and yet end up wanting to determine how they should live in the area where they live and want to spread their morals in public; this is also politics.

There are well-known examples of strikes carried out by members of a particular faith seeking change in the state, to the extent that they support certain people to lead the country in their wished favor.

The world has many practical examples of faith that govern nations. It would not be surprising to ignore the strong ties between Religion and politics. Understanding the role of religions and beliefs in political decision-making and recognizing the role of politics in determining beliefs is the key to giving policy a clear direction.

After all, the politics of a particular country should not be against any specific beliefs. If such a belief favors people to live in harmony and peacefully because being against some thoughts is the beginning of discrimination, and a particular religion is not just a name or a symbol but a plurality of members. Also, a specific belief should be consistent with the country's politics because the nation looks after the interests of all citizens in general and not a particular member of a specific faith.

In any case, the people we need have a peaceful development on our land that forever gives hope to our descendants. The goals of a particular religion should be in harmony with God's good purpose for humankind through the administration of the state. In any case, our religious principles should not interfere with the other person's needs. A person needs the good that sustains him in peace for a lifetime; this is what good politics should do for people.

Politics is our life, so we should not play with our lives. All you see is not compassion, and some are not an accident, but your political choices determine your life today. At the same time, you should understand that the government should only sometimes ask you to abide by its policies because a health policy is in the people's best interests. It, therefore, leads to the control and understanding of good politics for the people in general, which requires someone to know the good needed to live well in peace and that of others forever.

Now you can be able to understand government programs and the vision and mission of particular religions; this helps to personally anticipate the good or bad outcome to decide whether to participate or not. For now, you have the entire package to get along well with people and anything that you socialize with them. I am sure that now if it is a time of conflict, you know the real way to get things back on track without hurting anyone or anything.

There is so much that is prepared in a big secret, yet it has a good or bad purpose for the people. I hope now you can discover good or bad intentions by asking yourself why this scene is and what is behind it. I am sure that it has helped you to have your own line of participation or adherence to every eye-catching or requested activity.

REFERENCES

1. Phillips, Anne, 'From a Politics of Ideas to a Politics of Presence?', The Politics of Presence (Oxford, 1998; online edn, Oxford Academic, 1 Nov. 2003), https://doi.org/10.1093/0198294158.003.0001, accessed 20 Jan. 2023.

2. S,Russell .H. Larson and P. Piot, (2007) Good Politics, Bad Politics: The Experience of AIDS PMCID: PMC2040384 PMID: 17901417. doi: 10.2105/AJPH.2007.121418.

3. Korman, Rémi. (2014). The Tutsi body in the 1994 genocide: Ideology, physical destruction, and memory. 10.7228/manchester/9780719096020.003.0010.

4. Małczyński, Jacek & Domańska, Ewa & Smykowski, Mikołaj & Kłos, Agnieszka. (2020). The Environmental History of the Holocaust. Journal of Genocide Research. 22. 1-14. 10.1080/14623528.2020.1715533.

5. Korman, Rémi. (2014). The Tutsi body in the 1994 genocide: Ideology, physical destruction, and memory. 10.7228/manchester/9780719096020.003.0010.

6. Małczyński, Jacek & Domańska, Ewa & Smykowski, Mikołaj & Kłos, Agnieszka. (2020). The Environmental History of the Holocaust. Journal of Genocide Research. 22. 1-14. 10.1080/14623528.2020.1715533.

7. P. Canivez (2004). Jean-Jacques Rousseau's Concept of People Volume 30, Issue 4 https://doi.org/10.1177/0191453704044025 full reference.

Such mistakes of limiting love among people are often made and fueled by bad politics of hatred, and divisions. This is not the first or last time you will hear great leaders talk about selfishness. You find that love only happens among citizens of a particular country; In other words, though others die and pass away, we live. These are the words and actions of a corrupt world.

It is regrettable now to find such discrimination in the country. Citizens are divided into ethnic, religious, or cultural backgrounds, and so the conflict starts, leading to murder and even Genocide. So the other corrupted culture in the world made some keep quiet, saying that if we are well and in peace, we don't care about others. And in such a way, some people begin to make a big mistake that they are the only people alive, and they dehumanize themselves by dehumanizing others. They go on and on until they put on the face of a mindless animal and turn others into worthless animals even though they no longer exist. However, everything is done to take life and destroy those they call their enemies.

THANK YOU!

LET'S MEET IN THE NEXT BOOK!